CONTENTS

WHO IS R L STINE? 4

BORN IN OHIO 8

TELL ME A STORY 10

THE BUDDING WRITER 12

SUNDIAL SUPREMO 14

INTO THE REAL WORLD 16

NEW YORK, NEW YORK! 18

SOFT DRINKS AND A SPOUSE 20

'A VERY LUCKY WRITER' 22

'HOW TO BE FUNNY' 24

AN ADDITION TO THE FAMILY 26

IN SEARCH OF WORK AGAIN 28

EUREEKA'S CASTLE 30

FROM COMEDY TO HORROR 32

THE BABY-SITTER 34

WHERE YOUR WORST NIGHTMARES LIVE 36

SPOOKING YOUNGER READERS 38

THE DESIRE FOR MASTERY 40

'A WRITING MACHINE' 42

MULTI-MEDIA MARVEL 44

READERS WRITE ABOUT STINE 46

R L STINE: FOR AND AGAINST 48

R L STINE – TIMELINE 52

FURTHER READING 53

GLOSSARY 54

INDEX 56

Who Is R L Stine?

RL Stine is one of the most successful authors of modern times, but as he himself likes to say, 'No one over the age of 14 knows who I am.' While this is not strictly true, he is certainly better known by younger than older readers. This is because almost all his books are written for children aged eight to thirteen. His books are extremely popular with boys and girls all over the world; by early 1999 there were 200 million copies of his books in print, in 16 different languages. Many of them belonged to two series that he created in the early 1990s: *Fear Street* and *Goosebumps*.

As the titles of these series suggest, Stine's books can best be described as 'scary'. But there is plenty of humour in them too – as you might expect from a man who used to write joke books for a living. 'There is the right balance between horror and humour,' Stine said in 1999. 'Adult-horror writers really want to scare their readers. But I don't. My books are more of a tease. If the horror starts getting too **intense**, I put in something funny… The main thing is that I really like kids. I know how to communicate with them. My books are easy to read because they are written in short chapters. Every chapter ends in a **cliff-hanger**. And it's always a shock, which kids love.'

HEINEMAN
Profi

R I

An Una

Sep 94

Bu

540

WORCESTERS
COU!

54

RfS

JB
STLN E
R

BROMSGROVE JUNIOR

Please return/renew this item by the last date shown

worcestershire
countycouncil
Cultural Services

700022605405

Haydn Middleton

Heinemann
LIBRARY

www.heinemann.co.uk.

Visit our website to find out more information about Heinemann Library books

To order:

☎ Phone ++44 (0)1865 888066

▤ Send a fax to ++44 (0)1865 314091

▢ Visit the Heinemann Bookshop at www.heinemann.co.uk to browse our catalogue and order online.

First published in Great Britain by Heinemann Library, Halley Court, Jordan Hill, Oxford OX2 8EJ, a division of Reed Educational and Professional Publishing Ltd. Heinemann is a registered trademark of Reed Educational & Professional Publishing Limited.

OXFORD MELBOURNE AUCKLAND JOHANNESBURG BLANTYRE GABORONE IBADAN PORTSMOUTH NH (USA) CHICAGO

© Reed Educational and Professional Publishing Ltd 2001
The moral right of the proprietor has been asserted.

All rights reserved. No part of this publication may be reproduced, stored in a retrieval system, or transmitted in any form or by any means, electronic, mechanical, photocopying, recording, or otherwise without either the prior written permission of the Publishers or a licence permitting restricted copying in the United Kingdom issued by the Copyright Licensing Agency Ltd, 90 Tottenham Court Road, London W1P OLP.

Designed by Visual Image
Originated by Dot Gradations
Printed and bound in Hong Kong/China

ISBN 0431 086389 (paperback) ISBN 0431 086311 (hardback)

06 05 04 03 02   06 05 04 03 02

10 9 8 7 6 5 4 3 2 1   10 9 8 7 6 5 4 3 2 1

British Library Cataloguing in Publication Data

Middleton, Haydn
R.L. Stine. – (Heinemann Profiles)
1. Stine, R.L. – Biography – Juvenile literature
2. Novelists, American – 20th century – Biography – Juvenile literature
I. Title
813.5'4

Acknowledgements

The Publishers would like to thank the following for permission to reproduce photographs:
Bettman Corbis p31; DC Comics p17; Image Bank pp8, 19; Kobal Collection pp12, 26, 45; Yiorgos Nikiteas pp6, 10, 11, 27, 34, 38, 43, 44, 50; Ohio State University Archives p15; Rex Features p37; Ronald Grant Archive p33; Scholastic Children's Books p5; Sygma/F.Veronsky pp20, 24, 28; Telegraph Colour Library p39.

Cover photograph reproduced with permission of Sygma/F.Veronsky

Every effort has been made to contact copyright holders of any material reproduced in this book. Any omissions will be rectified in subsequent printings if notice is given to the Publisher.

Any words appearing in the text in bold, **like this**, are explained in the Glossary.

R. L. Stine has gone from writing joke books to becoming a master of horror.

MULTI-MEDIA SUCCESS

It is hard to exaggerate Stine's success as a children's author. A 1999 survey of books borrowed from British libraries, for example, showed that nine out of the top ten titles were his. But he is massively popular in other **media** too: The *Goosebumps* TV show – launched in 1995 – draws huge audiences, as do one-hour TV specials; videos based on the shows have sold in their millions; a movie is being made by Fox Family Films; the Disney Organization has set

A selection of Goosebumps **merchandising** products.

up a *Goosebumps* Horror Land at its MGM Studios site in Florida; and a live *Goosebumps* 'stage spectacular' tour of the USA started in autumn 1998.

Stine's stories and characters provide wonderfully exciting material for today's entertainment industry, whatever the country, and whatever language is spoken there. The **critic** Patrick Jones remarked, 'He is not interested in educating, enlightening or informing; he is only interested in entertaining by terrifying with gruesome plot-twisting scary thrillers for kids... He uses humour, roller-coaster plots, suspenseful chapter endings, gross-outs, credible kids, dialogue, recognizable if **stereotypical** characters, **cliff-hangers** and red herrings, and a bare bones style to get to the point: to scare his readers.' Millions of children worldwide – boys and girls alike – would agree that he gets to that point over and over and over again.

IS THERE A DOWNSIDE?

Not all adults, however, believe that R L Stine is a 'good thing'. Some say his books are not very well written, and that children deserve finer stories than his shock fiction. 'Teachers and parents have become increasingly concerned,' said the *New York Times* in 1997, 'that the books and their elaborate jackets contain **satanic** symbols, promote disrespect for adults and encourage children to imagine disfigured bodies, lurking menaces and, well, vomit.'

Two years earlier, in a widely published article, Diana West bitterly attacked Stine's 'push-button characters' and plots that were simply 'a series of shocks occurring at absurdly frequent intervals.' She described his books as typical of late-20th-century 'shock culture… all sensation and no feeling', and blamed them for '**desensitizing** the very young, stunting the life of the mind before it has even begun.' The debate on the true value of R L Stine's scary fiction is still in full swing. Meanwhile, his books keep selling by the truckload.

'To the literary critics, Stine's books' **formulaic** nature may be a weakness, but in business terms it is clearly a strength. Stine has found a theme and, like a composer, he provides umpteen variations upon it, providing his audience with something exciting and new yet essentially familiar… For too long parents have whinged about children wasting their time on television, records, videos, computer games, drugs. Now, horror of horrors, they are reading books.'
Brian Pendreigh in *The Scotsman*, February 1997

Born in Ohio

Robert Lawrence Stine was born in Columbus, Ohio, on 8 October 1943. His father worked for a restaurant supply company, while his mother stayed at home to look after her three children: Robert – called Bob – who was the eldest, Bill and Pam. They lived in Bexley, a suburb of Columbus, in a tiny house three doors from the railroad tracks. 'We were surrounded by big houses owned by wealthy people,' Stine recalls. 'I felt like an outsider.' That was a promising start. Many other famous authors similarly felt that they did not quite fit in when they were young. This sense of being an outsider often encourages people to observe their world closely – and maybe then write down their impressions.

Columbus, the capital of Ohio, where Stine grew up.

'You can do it! jump!'

In 1997 Stine told the story of his life to his friend
Joe Arthur and it was published under the title, *It
Came From Ohio!* In it, Stine described his ordinary,
rather uneventful childhood. His family had no TV
until he was nine years old, so he spent hours
listening to the radio. He particularly enjoyed tuning
in to stations broadcasting from New York City.

Every night a storyteller called Jean Shepherd would
tell fascinating, funny tales about his boyhood, his
family and his friends. Stine learned a lot about
putting stories together from listening to Shepherd;
he also longed to live in New York himself one day,
and see the places that figured in these stories.

One incident from that period of his life lodged in
his memory. His parents sent him to day-camp one
summer. As a swimming beginner, Stine had won his
Tadpole badge. Next he had to go for the Turtle. For
that he had to jump into the pool, swim to the other
side, then swim back. He knew that the swimming
part would be no problem for him. But the idea of
jumping in scared him half to death. As it came
closer and closer to his turn, he froze – and although
everyone was yelling for him to go ahead and jump,
he turned and walked away in total panic. 'I think
back to that moment whenever I write about a kid
who is really terrified,' he told Joe Arthur years later.
'I remember how I felt – and I try to write that
same feeling of fear into my character.'

Tell Me a Story

As a child Stine was a keen reader. But even before he entered the world of books by himself, his mother stirred his interest in stories by reading him fairy tales, folktales and myths. One story that made a great impression on him was *The Adventures of Pinocchio* by Carlo Collodi. The Walt Disney film about the same character was nowhere near as gruesome as the original book.

In the original story, there is a scene where Pinocchio puts his feet on the stove and falls asleep. Being made of wood, he catches fire and his feet are burned off. Later in the story, when Pinocchio gets tired of Jiminy Cricket's advice, he takes a hammer and smashes him against the wall. It is this combination of danger, horror and comedy, with a hint of the fantastic, that Stine has incorporated into his own stories.

Stine devoured humorous writing of all kinds as a boy.

Why was his hair always so short?

Before he was ten, Stine was discovering the joys of science fiction. His favourite authors in this genre were Ray Bradbury, Robert Sheckley and Isaac Asimov. Books by these authors showed him the thrills of fantastical, imaginative stories. But his appetite for humour was equally large, and this was met by *Mad* magazine and horror comics.

Stine's mother thought the horror comics were trash and forbade him to bring them into the house. Stine got around this by reading them at the barbershop. He got a haircut every week!

He read 'proper' books, too – *Huckleberry Finn* by Mark Twain, the humorous novels of Max Shulman, the stories of James Thurber, and the hilarious novels of the British author P G Wodehouse, whom Stine still describes as his 'all-time favourite author'. He loved these books so much that by the age of nine he was determined to be a writer himself when he grew up.

Two classic sci-fi novels that enthralled 1960s readers.

THE BUDDING WRITER

At school Stine did well at **academic** subjects but he was no athlete. He liked to play softball but was useless at it. Although he was tall, he was no better at football or basketball, and one day when he was bowling he dropped the ball on his foot and broke his little toe. Although he loved sports, he was best suited to watching them on television.

He spent a lot of his free time alone in his room, writing stories and making little joke magazines and comics. His first production was *The All New Bob Stine Giggle Book,* using an old typewriter that he found in the attic, pens, pencils, crayons, paste, scissors and a stapler. Many more magazines followed, enjoyed by his brother Bill and his friends at school. Stine did all the drawings as well as the text. He admits now that he was hardly a great artist!

As a boy, Stine loved to watch films like *It Came from Beneath the Sea.*

THE FUTURE BECOMES CLEAR

Stine's family was Jewish and just before he turned thirteen he began, like all Jewish boys, to prepare for his **Bar Mitzvah**. When his parents asked him what Bar Mitzvah gift he wanted, he simply asked for a new and better typewriter. Armed with that, he produced new and better magazines with titles like *Whammy* and *From Here to Insanity*.

He got a huge thrill from entertaining his friends with his funny writing. He later told students in an online interview in 1998, 'I started writing when I was nine… I don't know why I found it so interesting. I've been writing ever since though; it's all I've ever done.' As he grew older, he never lost his knack of appealing to young readers. He also looked more closely at what he liked in other writers' books and tried to learn from it. 'I liked surprise endings so much when I was a kid,' he told Joe Arthur. 'I remembered them when I started writing scary books. I decided I wanted to have a surprise at the end of every book. Then I decided it would be even *more* fun to have a surprise at the end of every *chapter*.'

Ted: I saw you pushing your bicycle to work.
Ned: I was so late I didn't have time to get on it.'
The best joke in Stine's first-ever self-produced comic book, c.1951, according to *It Came from Ohio!*

SUNDIAL SUPREMO

Atter high school, Stine won a place at college to study English. He chose to attend Ohio State University, which was just a bus ride away from his home. Some students prefer to open their wings and 'flee the nest' at this stage of their lives. Stine, however, wanted to keep living at home and enjoying his mother's cooking. But there was another reason why he chose Ohio State: it ran a humorous magazine called *Sundial*, for which his hero James Thurber once wrote and the famous artist Milton Caniff once drew.

'JOVIAL BOB'

In between classes, Stine spent almost all his time working for *Sundial*. He joined the staff at the beginning of his first year at university, and at the end of it he was made the **editor**. He kept the job for three years. People around the campus knew him then as 'Jovial Bob' – a name he made up for himself because he wanted someone with this name to be a running character in the magazine. 'In fact,' he says, 'I liked to think of myself as a running joke.'

Stine's childhood experience of making comics was extremely valuable now. Each month, for 25 cents an issue, he made sure that Ohio State's students received a magazine packed with cartoons, fake interviews and **spoof** advertisements. Sometimes,

Ohio State University in Columbus, where Stine spent his college years.

too, *Sundial's* writers pointed out aspects of college life that were unfair – like earlier **curfew** times for women than men – and campaigned for a fairer deal. Stine loved every minute of his editorship, but in June 1965 it all came to an end. That was when he graduated – and had to look for a proper job.

Sometimes the *Lantern*, Ohio State's student newspaper, was critical of Stine and the *Sundial*. After one attack, the *Sundial* printed this letter:

'Dear *Lantern* Editor:

I want to take this opportunity to defend *Sundial* and Jovial Bob Stine from the attack in last Wednesday's letter column. The *Sundial* is a constantly improving enterprise, and Jovial Bob is a man of infinite wit and talent ... I would have made these same statements even if my brother hadn't forced me.

H. William Stine' (Stine's brother, Bill)

From *It Came from Ohio!*

Into the Real World

Stine still nursed his childhood ambition to live in New York. Ideally, he also wanted to write for a top magazine. But New York was one of the world's most expensive cities in which to live, and Stine had precious little money saved up from his time at college. So he stayed at home for the launch of his career – not as a writer, but as a **substitute teacher** for a year.

He now calls it the toughest job he ever had. But he enjoyed the experience, and he learned a great deal himself. Teaching gave him the chance to watch kids in action. Many children's authors are former teachers – being constantly around children gives them a better idea of how they talk and how they act. They are able to write stories that are more true to life. Stine feels that his year as a teacher was invaluable to his career as a children's author. Sometimes, when starting a new book, he remembers some of his former students for inspiration.

Captain Anything

When Stine was not preparing lessons or marking students' work, he worked on a new writing project. He had loved listening to the radio as a boy, and now he produced some radio scripts of his own. His idea was to create 2-minute radio programmes about a character called *Captain Anything*. This superhero

could change into any kind of animal, mineral or vegetable – but his horn-rimmed glasses would always remain. So, for example, if Captain Anything turned into a lettuce, he would be a lettuce in horn-rimmed spectacles!

With some friends – and the help of two Columbus radio personalities – Stine made records of four sample episodes which he sent to radio stations all over the USA. It seemed that the **commercial** writing career of Robert Lawrence Stine was about to take off.

Sometimes Stine gave his students 'free reading' periods – they could even read comic books!

But it was not to be. As Stine says, the same answer kept coming back: no one was interested. He was by no means the first would-be writer to suffer an early setback. How different things would have been if, like some, Stine had been too crushed by **rejection** to keep trying!

New York, New York!

Ayear after graduating, at least one part of Stine's dream came true – he moved to New York. He had saved enough money to put down a **deposit** on a single-room apartment. On arriving in the big city, he had to get a job so he could pay the rent. He scanned the advertisements, hoping to find work in the magazine world. In 1966 the top titles were **glossies** like *Life*, *Esquire* and *The New Yorker*. But an unknown lad from Columbus could not expect to start there.

Investors and invention

His first job was a specialist magazine near Wall Street, called *Institutional Investor*. Stine knew nothing about **stocks and shares**, but that was only half his problem. He was employed on the magazine's **production** side, not to do any of the writing. It soon became clear that although he had helped to produce the *Sundial* at college, Stine did not have the necessary production skills. For this reason he did not work for *Institutional Investor* for long.

Stine's next job was just as demanding, but in a rather different way. He worked for the editor of six teenage fan magazines. One of them was called *Country & Western Music*. On his first day, Stine was asked to write an interview with country star Glen Campbell. But instead of actually asking Campbell questions, he was expected to read newspaper clippings about him – then make all the answers up! Amazingly, stars never sued the magazines, his boss told him: 'they don't care what you write about them – as long as you keep writing about them.'

Over the next month Stine 'interviewed' the Beatles, Supremes, Tom Jones and many others in exactly the same way. It came very easily to him, since he had such a vivid imagination. He also persuaded his boss to start up a new magazine, *Adventures in Horror*, and in it he published his first horror story: 'Bony Fingers From the Grave' under the name of Robert Lawrence.

But then the company went bust, and Stine had to search for yet another job.

Greenwich Village in 1960s New York, where Stine lived as a young writer.

Soft Drinks and a Spouse

If one day you plan to be a writer, it is useful to do a number of different jobs. At the very least the experience can give you something to write about later. But Stine found his next post boring at the time, and boring to look back on. He was employed by a magazine called *Soft Drink Industry*. Now, instead of reading clippings and making up celebrity interviews he had to read clippings and write articles

Stine's wife Jane proved to be a partner in business as well as in life.

about soft drinks, soda cans, syrups and their containers. One spell-binding article, he remembers, was entitled 'New American Flange Hopper Speeds Feeding Of Rip Cap Closures.'

But however dull the subject matter was, Stine certainly learned how to write fast: 'I would have to do twenty articles a day… It taught me not to stop and think about it. I just had to sit down and write.' This would prove to be a valuable skill in years to come.

CHANGES ON THE HOME FRONT

Meanwhile, back in Columbus, Stine's father retired. With his wife and daughter Pam he moved out to northern California. 'In the back of my mind,' Stine told Joe Arthur, 'I knew that it meant that my childhood home was gone. I was truly on my own in New York.'

This was not strictly true. Stine had friends in the city – girlfriends, too. One of them, Jane Waldhorn, was just out of college. Stine met her at a party in Brooklyn, started going out with her and soon they decided to get married. He had enjoyed a very secure home life as a child. Now he was going to build the same kind of security with his partner. He still calls her 'the smartest person I know', and her smartness was to play a vital part in his later success as a writer of books for children. But in 1969, the year of their marriage, Stine had just started another magazine job – as a staff writer for *Junior Scholastic*.

'A Very Lucky Writer'

In December 1968 Stine settled into a tiny office at Scholastic Inc. His job was to write news and history articles for *Junior Scholastic*, a national weekly magazine. Until now, he had flitted from job to job like a butterfly – but he was destined to stay with this firm for no fewer than sixteen years.

Had Stine's dream come true?

As a boy Stine had dreamed of living in New York and writing and editing magazines. Now he was doing just that. Some people can be disappointed by getting exactly what they want in life. Not Robert Stine. He had the time of his life – working on four magazines **simultaneously**: planning one issue, writing another, editing a third, **proof-reading** a fourth.

Working in children's publishing is a job that requires teamwork and creativity.

'Magazine writing was the perfect training for me. I learned to write fast – and move on to the next piece. I'm a very lucky writer. I've always been able to write quickly, and it usually comes out the way I want it on the first try… Kids always ask me what I do about **writer's block**. I have to confess that I've never had it. I can always sit down and write. When you are writing for magazines, there's no time for writer's block!'

From *It Came From Ohio!* 1997

WHAT WAS JANE DOING?

For a while both Stine and his wife worked at Scholastic. But Jane left to become the editor of *Dynamite*, a massively popular monthly magazine for children, full of interviews, jokes, puzzles and posters. One word that described its contents was 'zany' – and so was the new monthly magazine for over-12s that Stine launched for Scholastic soon afterwards, in 1975. Called *Bananas*, it ran articles with titles like HOW TO TURN YOUR POEMS INTO DOG FOOD, and featured a character named Phil – 'America's Most Beloved Fly'.

Bananas became extremely successful – and not just among teenaged readers. One adult who found the magazine hilarious was Ellen Rudin, a children's book editor at the firm of E P Dutton. She rang Stine with a proposition…

'How to Be Funny'

Ellen Rudin liked Stine's sense of humour so much, she wanted him to try to write a funny book for children. Without her suggestion, Stine might never have entered the world of children's literature. He had not given much thought to book-writing before, but now he gave it a shot. The result was *How To Be Funny* – a guide to being funny in all sorts of situations. E P Dutton were impressed, and agreed to publish it. Stine was about to step onto the road to fame and fortune. Or was he?

Though Stine started by writing humour books, he soon switched from rabbit ears to skeletons!

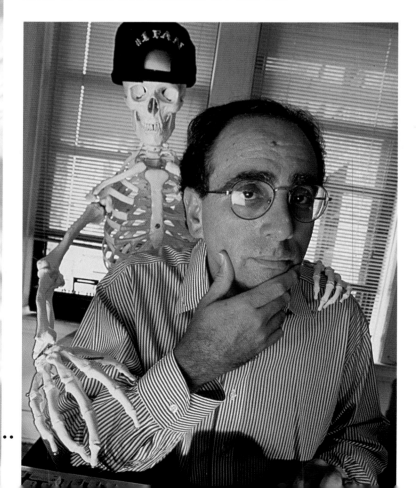

'Part One: Recognizing a Joke

Here are three items. Only one of them is a joke. Circle the number of the item you believe to be a joke.

1 "Fire! Help! Fire!"

2 "Help! Police! I'm being robbed!"

3 "Boy, am I glad to come in out of the snoo."

"Snoo? What's snoo?"

"Nothing. What's snoo with you?"'

From *How To Be Funny*, 1978

WHERE ARE THE CROWDS?

When the book came out, Stine's sister-in-law organized a **book-signing** at the bookstore on Fifth Avenue where she worked. Stine sat at a desk beside piles of his book wearing bunny rabbit ears. (Since he was being advertised as 'Jovial Bob Stine', he thought he should look the part.) It turned out to be an embarrassing session. Only one person came up to the desk, bought a copy of the book and asked the author to sign his autograph.

It was not a very promising start. But in time the book sold better, and when Stine later became a literary phenomenon with *Fear Street* and *Goosebumps*, fans turned up to his signings in their thousands. Meanwhile Stine continued the good work on *Bananas* magazine – and if things got a little quiet in the Scholastic offices, he kept the staff on their toes by sending **spoof** memos. One advised everyone to wear raincoats to work the next day, since the overhead sprinkler system was going to be tested!

An Addition
to the Family

In April 1999, long after Stine had become the biggest seller in children's fiction, British journalist Alasdair Riley asked him why he thought he had been so successful. 'The main thing is that I really like kids,' he replied. 'I know how to communicate with them.' Some **critics** say that Stine is on the same wavelength as so many children because he has never really grown up himself. Thus he not only shares their wacky sense of humour, he also sees the world in the same way that they do. But the best way to stay in touch with children's tastes is to spend

Stine and his son loved to watch old films featuring the comic duo Stan Laurel (right) and Oliver Hardy.

a lot of time with them – and from 7 June 1980 Stine had a child of his very own for company: a son named Matthew Daniel.

Just as Stine's own family in Columbus had been very close, so he, Jane and Matthew also became a very tight little unit. (Perhaps as a result of this the boy heroes and girl heroines in Stine's *Goosebumps* books usually live in houses with both

Stine's son Matt is the boy on the cover of this Fear Street book.

their parents – they do not come from broken homes.) When Matthew ('Matt') was little, he and his father would do lots of things together – explore New York City, watch old *Laurel and Hardy* films, play ball in the park – and generally enjoy each other's company.

WHY WON'T HE READ MY BOOKS?

As Matt grew older, he preferred to spend time playing his guitar and hanging out with his friends – but he and Stine remain good friends. The author must have learned a lot during his son's boyhood years about what children enjoy. Matt, however, is not sure if he enjoys his father's books. This is because he has never read a single one! 'He never would,' Stine told an interviewer in 1998. 'And now he's too old for them… Even the one I put him in, he didn't read. He's the star of *Goodnight Kiss*, the *Fear Street* vampire book, and he wouldn't even read that one. And he was on the cover of *The Perfect Date*… but he didn't read it… Every writer I know, their kids don't read their stuff. It's like a natural way for kids to rebel.' Stine himself, by contrast, seems not to have rebelled very hard as a child. Maybe that helps to explain why he became so keen to cause shock and horror in his books after he grew up!

In Search of Work Again

One sure thing about the world of children's literature – whether magazines or books – is that tastes do not stay the same for ever. Stine discovered this at Scholastic Inc as the 1970s turned into the 1980s.

His magazine *Bananas*, which had once been so popular, successful and 'cool', was now selling in smaller numbers than before. In 1984 Scholastic

Stine was writing books for children long before Goosebumps came along – or his spooky new look!

decided to stop publishing it. Stine was made editor of another magazine, *Maniac*, but that lasted for only a year and then the company re-organized. As a result, Stine lost his job.

How did he make ends meet?

Stine was in a better position than many men who become unemployed in their early 40s. His wife Jane and her friend Joan Waricha formed their own publishing company – Parachute Press, Inc. – which was to become very successful. Also, Stine was not exactly unemployed. Already, after *How To Be Funny*, he was writing funny children's books for several different publishers. Being at home all the time just meant that he could devote more time to these projects – and, of course, hang out with Matt.

In *It Came From Ohio!*, Stine lists the many varied writing **assignments** that he took on at this time. They included some 'Find-Your-Fate' books about Indiana Jones and James Bond – each of which had 25 different endings that the reader could choose from. There were also some G.I. Joe adventure novels ('even though I didn't know a rifle from a golf club!'), and a series of books about a bunch of rubber balls with faces. He even wrote the single line of text at the foot of each page of *Mighty Mouse* colouring books.

In fact, Stine got so busy that he switched at last from his trusty old typewriter and started to write on a computer – to speed things up.

Eureeka's Castle

Until self-employed writers strike it rich, they often have to take whatever work is offered. They have to be **adaptable**, and prepared to work in other **media**, too. Soon after graduating Stine had tried his hand – in vain – at writing for radio. Now, with more experience behind him, he was given a chance to write for TV.

The show was for Nickelodeon, the US cable channel, and it was called *Eureeka's Castle*. Its audience was pre-school children, like the audience for *Sesame Street*, but *Eureeka's Castle* was not educational, just fun. Stine was made head writer for the puppet sketches, with ten other writers to help him.

Learning how to work in a team

Stine and his staff wrote a hundred hours of scripts for the programme, and also four half-hour specials. Kids loved it – and after its first season it won an Ace Award as top children's show. Stine soon discovered that writing for TV is a group activity. Scripts are constantly rewritten as all the writers make suggestions. One advantage of working with a group is that there are more people to think up jokes – the disadvantage is that not everyone thinks they are funny! And once a script is complete, there is nothing to stop actors from saying whatever they want.

Like many writers, Stine was often inspired by other people – like writer James Thurber as well as his own son.

But teamwork has a part to play in most kinds of writing. Very rarely does a writer have an idea for a story, write it up, then see it published without a word being changed. Stine himself said in an interview on the *Goosebumps* website that he got 'lots of help from my editors, my readers and my friends.' Stine is an author who appreciates **feedback** on his work, and is prepared to make changes if he agrees with the suggestions of people he trusts.

Writers also need to look to others sometimes to gather their material. A crazy bat in *Eureeka's Castle*, Batly, kept flying into walls or falling down steps then saying 'I *meant* to do that!' Stine had heard his son Matt say just the same thing whenever he fell over as a toddler!

From Comedy to Horror

As a child Stine had loved to scare himself by reading horror books. As an adult he had continued to enjoy reading horror fiction. But until 1986 he had never written and published a horror novel of his own. And he might never have done so at all, if an old friend at Scholastic had not invited him to have a try. (In book-writing – as in most other kinds of work – it helps to have 'friends in high places' who can help to move your career along!)

What's in a title?

Stine's friend at Scholastic, Jean Feiwel, suggested he should write his scary story for 'Young Adults' (YA). Publishers like to make sure that writers have a particular **target readership** in mind. She also suggested a title that Stine could use: *Blind Date* (not to be confused with the TV show of the same name).

Stine did a little research, checking out how many other scary YA books were on sale (very few), and getting a feel for the **genre**. Afterwards he spent a month working on an outline for *Blind Date*, and three more months writing it. The story was about a boy who got phone calls from a mysterious girl who had been dead for three years. Jane gave Stine a great deal of help in improving it. Then the team at Scholastic polished it up and published it.

Stine claims now that he was surprised – but *Blind Date* immediately became a bestseller. Scholastic felt that YA readers were ready for more novels in the same style, so they asked Stine to write a second novel: *Twisted*, which also did well. That was followed shortly afterwards by a third, *The Baby-sitter*.

Stine enjoyed reading horror books for adults, by authors like Stephen King – shown here with a feline fan – but there were few scary books for YA readers.

'Unlike most authors, Stine thinks of the title first... "I think up titles while I'm walking the dog. Recently, we held a nationwide competition for kids in America to come up with a good title. The winner was *Dead Dogs Still Fetch*, but I don't think we'll get a good book out of that." '

Stine talking to Alasdair Riley, *The Times*, 23 April 1999

THE BABY-SITTER

S tine's third YA scary novel, *The Baby-sitter*, was published in the USA in 1989. (It was published in the UK two years later. Most books tend to be published first in the author's home country, and elsewhere only later.) It was based on Stine's own fears as a baby-sitter when he was younger and, like the other two novels, it sold extremely well. Stine had already hit upon a **distinctive** way of writing horror fiction that left his readers gasping for more. Once he had found this **formula**, he had little need to depart from it in later books.

The cover of R L Stine's third scary novel for YA readers.

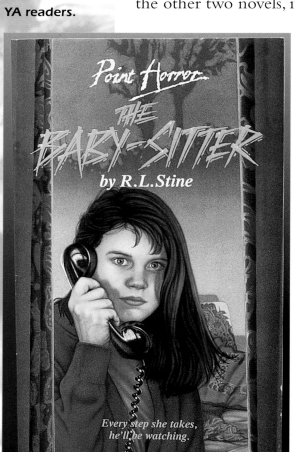

Point Horror
THE BABY-SITTER
by R.L.Stine

Every step she takes, he'll be watching.

WHO'S THAT KNOCKING AT THE WINDOW?

The atmosphere in *The Baby-sitter* is tense throughout. Jenny has a vivid imagination, and often succeeds in spooking herself. But when she starts to baby-sit for a new family in town, someone else is definitely trying to do the spooking. Who is it? Chuck from school who wants to be her boyfriend but has a slightly creepy sense of humour? The mysterious Mr Willers who says he lives next door, even though the house is empty? Or is it the last guy on earth that Jenny would have imagined? Stine keeps you guessing right to the end.

But *The Baby-sitter*, like Stine's other YA horror novels, is not just about scares. There is quite a lot of love-interest as Jenny decides whether or not to go out with Chuck. And since 'Jovial Bob' is the author, there are several pretty good jokes. Stine also manages to convince the reader that he really understands how teenagers think – as you can see from this short passage:

'Maybe I'll go in and get my nose pierced,' [said Jenny's friend, Laura]

'You can't,' Jenny said, pulling her past the store. 'You need a parent's permission if you're under eighteen.'

'How do you know?'

'Ellen Sappers tried to get her ears pierced in three stores a few weeks ago, and they wouldn't do it without a note from her mother.'

'Did she get the note?'

'No way. Ellen said that if her mother approved of it, she didn't want to do it.'

From Chapter 9 of *The Baby-sitter*, 1989

WHERE YOUR WORST NIGHTMARES LIVE

S tine began to get letters from his readers, asking for more scary books. 'After 23 years of writing, I had found something that readers *really liked*,' he modestly says. There was a popular demand, and Stine wanted to meet it. He began to wonder if he should write a *series* of scary books: each book would make perfect sense on its own, but all of them would be set in the same place. This would help readers to know exactly what they were buying (and booksellers to know exactly what they were **stocking**). It might also encourage readers to 'collect the set' of these books, so raising more **royalties** for Stine!

WHAT DID JANE THINK?

As usual, Stine talked over the whole project with his wife Jane, who liked it a lot. So did Jane's partner at Parachute Press, Joan Waricha. They were prepared to put the idea to Pat Macdonald, an editor at Pocket Books. But first they needed a good, strong title for the series – so Stine put his thinking cap on.

The title he came up with was *Fear Street*. When he told it to Jane, she added almost at once the follow-up line: 'Where your worst nightmares live.' She and Joan then convinced Pat Macdonald to sign up three

British author Agatha Christie – one of R L Stine's all-time favourites.

titles to launch the series. Stine set to work and the books started appearing in the shops in 1989: first *The New Girl*, then *The Surprise Party*, then *The Overnight*. Each one stormed up the bestseller lists. And since Stine's readers and his publishers wanted more, more, more – that was what he gave them. Now that he had hit his stride, there was no stopping him. Soon he was writing a new *Fear Street* every month.

The rest, as they say, is history. By mid-1999 Stine had written so many *Fear Streets* that there were now many different sub-groups within the series, too. These included the 'Fear Street Saga' books, 'Ghosts of Fear Street' books, and – from June 1998 – 'Fear Street Seniors', which follows the senior class at Shadyside High as they try to get through their 'killer' senior year.

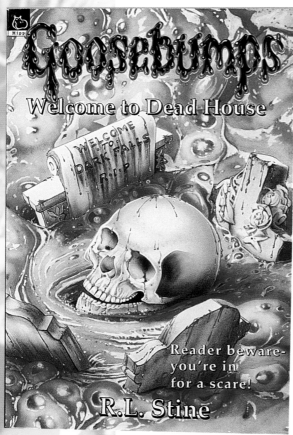

A typical cover for one of Stine's *Goosebumps* books that was published in Britain.

Before *Fear Street*, not many scary books had been written for young adults – and none with such success. This made Stine, his wife Jane and Joan Waricha wonder whether even *younger* readers might like to be spooked on a regular basis. Stine decided to find out, but before he started writing stories for children between seven and eleven years of age, he tried to come up with a good series title.

This time, it did not come so fast. He racked his brains until one day, while he was reading the TV listings in *TV Guide*, he saw an advert for a week of scary movies on Channel 11. The headline said: 'It's GOOSEBUMPS Week on Channel 11!' Stine called Jane at once: ' "Here it is! The title for the new book series!" I cried. "We'll call it *Channel 11*!" Just kidding. Of course we called it *Goosebumps*.'

A visit to the Tower of London gave Stine the inspiration for *A Night in Terror Tower,* one of his *Goosebumps* books.

WAS *Goosebumps* AN INSTANT SUCCESS?

Not only did Stine now have a series title – he had also dreamed up a title for the first book: *Welcome to Dead House.* He wrote that story in just ten days. When it was published, it didn't set the world on fire at once. Nor did the follow-up, *Stay Out of the Basement.* They did not sell badly of course, but it was not until the third book, *Monster Blood,* that sales began to rocket.

By then children were creating their own **buzz** about the books. Here was a series that gave you the same kind of thrills as a roller-coaster ride – but you still felt safe all the time. There was no blood, no guts, no bullets, no guns. There was also a lot more humour than in the *Fear Street* series.

Goosebumps were short, fun, easy to read, and as soon as you finished reading one, you wanted to go on to the next one. That was why at the end of each book there was a 'taster' of a few pages from another *Goosebumps* story. The children of the USA, and soon of the world, were hooked.

The Desire for Mastery

Unlike *Fear Street*, the *Goosebumps* stories were not all set in the same place. There was no central set of characters either. But children loved the 'safe scares' inside each book. By the sixth title, *Let's Get Invisible*, *Goosebumps* had cracked the children's bestseller list in *Publisher's Weekly* magazine. And by 1994, the bestseller list of *USA Today* (which includes adult as well as children's literature) showed that Stine had become the country's top seller. From then, it was only a matter of time before *Goosebumps* went worldwide. By 1999 more than 200 million of them were in print in 16 different languages.

Why does Stine think *Goosebumps* is so popular?

Stine believes that children like his stories because there are so many twists and surprises in each book. He also said in a 1998 interview with HomeArts: 'Kids all want mastery. They want mastery over their lives… The books all feature normal kids, kids who aren't interesting or special in any way – they're not talented, they're not brilliant, they're not anything. They are average kids, but they have to face horrible things. And their parents never help them; their parents are useless. The kids have to use their own wits and their imaginations and have to solve these problems, and they always do. There are always happy endings. And I think the kids really like that – the process of mastery, and that final victory.' It also helped that there were so many *Goosebumps* titles for children to collect – just as they had once collected Cabbage Patch Dolls or Power Rangers.

The substance inside the tin was bright green. It shimmered like jelly in the light from the overhead lamp.

"Touch it," Andy said.

But before Evan had a chance, she reached a finger in and poked it. "It's cold," she said. "Touch it. It's really cold."

Evan poked it with his finger. It was cold, thicker than jelly, heavier.

He pushed his finger beneath the surface. When he pulled his finger out, it made a loud sucking noise.

"Gross," Andy said.'

From *Monster Blood*, by R L Stine (1992)

Goosebumps everywhere

Fans of *Goosebumps* do not have to limit themselves to books and videos. There are many products that take advantage of the series' popularity to gain sales. There are *Goosebumps* notebooks, folders, skateboards, sports equipment, and even a *Goosebumps* board game. Pepsi and Fruti-Lay even ran a special scheme where children could collect coupons from the Pepsi cans and Doritos packets. They were to send these in to recieve a special *Goosebumps* book which was not available in bookstores. Some parents were upset that children were encouraged to buy 'junk food' in this way, but others were happy to see children reading, no matter what the reason.

'A Writing Machine'

Stine and his editors now had two hit series on their hands. Both *Fear Street* and *Goosebumps* had created a huge appetite for scary books – and only Stine could satisfy it. Some authors might have felt worried by this need to write more and more. Others might have demanded more free time, to enjoy the fruits of their success. But Stine met the challenge by making himself write faster. No longer could he spend long, hard months working on a book, as he had with *Blind Date*. Now he measured out the time in weeks – even days.

How does he do it?

One of the commonest questions Stine is asked is: how long does it take you to write a book? His answer, in 1997, was ten days for a *Fear Street* and eight days for a *Goosebumps*. Before that, he would spend two to three days working on the outline for each book. He regularly writes for six days a week, seven if he has to. In 1999 he told Alasdair Riley: 'I have written 85 [*Goosebumps*] since 1992. I have another 17 to go to complete my contract in a year and a half's time. Then I might get a life.'

He has no trouble switching between styles for the different series. In 1995 he even found the time to write an adult novel too: *Superstitious*. He claims that he did not really want to write the book, but was 'made an offer he could not refuse'. Amazingly, his son Matt showed great interest in this project – but after two chapters he gave up reading it. The **critics** and reviewers were not very happy with it either; but it still sold 150,000 copies and won a film deal.

In 1997, for the first time, sales of Stine's books began to slow down. His phenomenal success could not have continued forever – children's tastes change, and authors cannot always change with them. He says he is looking forward to working less hard, when *Fear Street* and *Goosebumps* lose all their appeal for young readers. In the meantime he continues to be 'a writing machine' – and according to him, 'this isn't any way for a human to live.'

THE WORLD'S BESTSELLING HORROR WRITER

R.L. STINE

SUPERSTITIOUS

The cover of Stine's only novel for adult readers – even if it looks more like a children's book!

MULTI-MEDIA MARVEL

Goosebumps is more than just the title of a book series. The **critic** Patrick Jones points out: 'The *Goosebumps* brand name appears on fast-food drink cups, snack foods, calendars, clothing, and everywhere else in the retail world. *Goosebumps* are ... popular culture products. From the movie tie-ins to the Cheetos bags, *Goosebumps* stopped being just books very soon into the series.' In this way children could buy the **merchandising** and get to know the brand-name without even reading a book by R L Stine.

The covers of Stine's videos are just as scary as his books!

Goosebumps ON SCREEN

Another way that children could get into *Goosebumps* was by watching TV and videos. The top-rating TV show began in 1995 – as a response to readers writing in and asking Stine when they could see his stories on screen. The first one to be shown on TV was *The Haunted Mask*: a terrifying tale about Carly Beth, a shy 11-year-old whose Halloween mask causes weird things to happen – until one day she finds that she cannot take it off...

In 1996 this story became the first *Goosebumps* available on video too.

A scene from *Jurassic Park* – one of the few films to scare R L Stine.

Not everyone thought it was harmless fun. 'If you plan to buy *The Haunted Mask*, watch your child's face as he or she watches it,' warned journalist John Larabee in *The Detroit News*. 'The video may be scaring the daylights out of the kid.'

Unlike some authors who feel that their work is ruined when it is filmed, Stine himself loves watching the shows – 'even the re-runs!' This is a little surprising. Once when he was asked, 'Why don't you have pictures in your books?' he replied, 'I think it's much scarier to imagine everything in your mind, and much more personal. An artist could never capture what YOU imagine.' But the covers of *Fear Street*, painted by Bill Schmidt, and those of *Goosebumps*, by Tim Jacobus, have played a big part in both series' success.

'Dear R.L. Stine,
I've read forty of your books – and I think they're really boring!'
One of Stine's favourite 'fan-mail' letters from the countless thousands he gets.

READERS WRITE
ABOUT STINE

'One of my favourite *Goosebumps* is *Bride of the Living Dummy*, sequel to Night of the Living Dummy. This time Slappy (the dummy) wants more: real revenge on Eddie, but the plot gets very twisted. I think it's a carefully-written book. It's not open-ended; every detail counts.'

Sarah, 11

'My favourite book is called *Calling All* Creeps. It's about a boy who plays a mean joke on someone but soon the joke's on him! It is a really well-written book and cleverly thought through and I think one of the best of the *Goosebumps* series.'

Daniel, 11

'*Cat* [a *Fear Street* title] is my best book by R L Stine. It's about a boy called Marty who kills a cat at basketball practice but he doesn't really mean to kill it. Marty keeps seeing the cat again and the cat seems to want to kill him.'

Olivia, 11

'*The Girlfriend* is about a boy called Scotty Singleton who has the perfect girlfriend called Lora, but when Lora goes away for the weekend he gets a new (horrible) girlfriend called Shannon, and she doesn't want to let him go when Lora returns. It is a very good book, cleverly written and it has a fabulous plot.'

Golnar, 11

'Stine's books have gone from being mildly entertaining to repetitive beyond belief. I don't think that anyone can deny that he is running out of ideas after *Night of the Living Dummy IV*. His storylines are hopelessly **clichéd**, but you can't expect much more from a man who knocks books out at the rate of one every two weeks… He has lost the power to surprise; you do nothing more in his books than wait for the 'revelation' that the killer is the quiet, unassuming one. Basically, once you've read one, you've read them all.'

Alex, 13

R L Stine:
For and Against

Millions of children love the work of R L Stine, but plenty of adults are not so enthusiastic. They find his writing slapdash, his plots feeble, his characters dull, and his string of grisly shocks just plain **juvenile**. As Diana West put it, in an attack on Stine in *The Weekly Standard* in 1995, 'the aim of all shock fiction is the same: to set off a bodily response which **debases** the act of reading – and, more importantly, the reader …'

Is Stine bad for children?

It is true that few adults can enjoy a *Fear Street* or *Goosebumps* story in the way that they might enjoy, say, *The Lion, the Witch and the Wardrobe* or a *Harry Potter* novel. But this is partly why Stine's books appeal to children. They feel that the author is interested in them, and in what they think – not in

These [Stine's] books do absolutely nothing to **edify** our children, or to promote decent morals, or kindness to one another.'

A parent from Lynn Haven, Florida, where a vote was taken on whether to keep Stine's books on school shelves or not.

what their parents or teachers think. So while adults worry about Stine's 'trashy' books, children want them even more. But this is nothing new. In more recent times, the hugely popular children's stories of Roald Dahl have upset some adults for much the same reasons.

These people believe that fiction for children should provide more than mere entertainment.

DOES *Goosebumps* SERVE ANY POSITIVE PURPOSE?

Stine's **detractors** are especially concerned about his Goosebumps series. That is because these books are for young children, who have not been reading for long and are still very easily influenced. But opinions on the issue seem to be changing, as Perry

'Long before anything resembling modern children's literature existed, parents and librarians were wringing their hands over children's reading lists. The early **Colonists** fussed about fairy tales. (Fantasy, they thought, strayed from Biblical teachings.) Nineteenth-century dime novels sparked concerns that the tales of fictional heroes, like Shorty Muldoon, were too physically stimulating and thus gave children a whiff of sexual awakening … Even series … like the Nancy Drew and Hardy Boys Mysteries were long snubbed by librarians as failing to provide moral lessons.

From *The New York Times*, 1997

No matter what their parents and teachers think, children continue to read R L Stine's books.

Nodelman pointed out in an article for the *Children's Literature Association Quarterly* late in 1997:

'When R L Stine's *Goosebumps* books first appeared, only a few years ago, many parents, teachers, and librarians viewed the mere existence of the new series as a monstrous intrusion into the well-intentioned world of children's publishing, and the content of the novels themselves as an equally monstrous intrusion into the ordinarily innocent minds of young readers. But as time has passed and the series has continued to be phenomenally popular with young readers, it becomes harder and harder to find adults willing to be more than mildly distressed by *Goosebumps*. When asked about children's apparently **insatiable** enthusiasm for these books, most adults I've spoken to lately tend to say something along the lines of, "Well, at least they're reading something."'

From his experience in publishing, Stine himself knows how hard it can be to get children to read. 'It's important,' he says, 'that kids should be able to discover they can turn to reading for entertainment instead of television or Nintendo.' He certainly succeeds in luring children into the world of literature where other authors have failed. And many of his fan letters give him the same message: 'I don't like books as a rule, but I really like yours.'

Maybe once children like these have been hooked by Stine, they may start to feel keener on other books too. But it is hard to imagine another modern author winning as much loyalty and respect from children as Robert Lawrence Stine – the man who spooked his way to record-breaking success.

'Parents seem to be really pleased, especially because their boys are reading… [Stine is] very good at coming up with today's language for kids. Today's styles, backgrounds, clothing… You hope for more quality, but get them into *Goosebumps* and maybe in the future they'll pick up Agatha Christie or Edgar Allan Poe.'
  Carl Winchman, a book specialist from Fargo, North Dakota, USA.

R L Stine – Timeline

1943	Robert Lawrence Stine born in Columbus, Ohio, USA
1951	Produces his first comic book – *The All New Bob Stine Giggle Book* – to distribute to his schoolmates
1956	Stine's parents give him a new typewriter as a gift for his Bar Mitzvah
1961	Enters Ohio State University and joins the staff of *Sundial*, the university's humour magazine
1962	Becomes editor of *Sundial*
1964	Stands for election as president of the student senate at Ohio State University, promising to 'do nothing' if elected. He loses the election.
1965	Works as a substitute teacher in Ohio for a year after graduating, becoming popular with the students when he lets them read comic books in class
1966	Moves to New York and starts a succession of jobs for various magazines, including *Soft Drink Industry*
1968	Starts work as a staff writer for the national weekly magazine *Junior Scholastic*
1969	Marries Jane Waldhorn
1975	Becomes editor of Scholastic magazine *Bananas*
1978	Publishes *How to Be Funny*, his first book. Attends his first book-signing wearing bunny rabbit ears.
1980	Son Matthew Daniel born
1983	Jane and her friend Joan Waricha leave their jobs at Scholastic to start Parachute Press
1985	Stine leaves Scholastic after *Bananas* is cancelled and writes at home for a living, including scripts for *Eureeka's Castle* TV show
1986	Publishes *Blind Date*, his first scary novel
1989	Publishes first novel in the *Fear Street* series

1992	Publishes first novels in the *Goosebumps* series
1993	*Goosebumps* books become best-sellers
1994	In a list of the year's best-selling books in the USA, 26 of the 234 titles are by Stine
1995	Launch of *Goosebumps* TV show in the United States
1996	Stine publishes first (and only) adult novel, *Superstitious*
1997	Sales of *Goosebumps* begin to slow down. Stine collaborates with Joe Arthur on *It Came From Ohio!*, about Stine's life. The *Goosebumps HorrorLand Fright Show* and *Fun House* opens at Disney-MGM Studios in Florida, USA.
1999	The stage show *Goosebumps Live* tours the UK
2000	Stine launches a new series called *The Nightmare Room*

FURTHER READING

McGwire, Scarlett. *Twentieth Century Issues: Censorship*. London: Hodder Wayland, 1999.

Thomas, Roger. *Magazines & Comics*. Oxford: Heinemann Library, 1999.

Graham, Ian. *Books and Newspapers*. London: Evans Brothers Ltd, 2000.

Stine R L, as Told To Joe Arthur. *It Came from Ohio!* New York: Scholastic, 1997.

GLOSSARY

activist person who actively works for change

academic scholarly

adaptable easily able to cope with new situations

assignment task

Bar Mitzvah introductory religious ceremony for Jewish boys of 13

book-signing public event where author autographs copies of his/her books

buzz widespread excitement that develops as one person tells another about something

cliff-hanger break in a story at a moment of uncertainty and excitement, which makes the reader desperate to read on and discover the outcome

clichéd commonly used; not orginal

Colonists the first Europeans to live in America

commercial money-making

critic person who analyzes one of the arts (literature or film, for example) and sometimes judges it

curfew time after which a person must be indoors

debase lower the quality of something

deposit initial payment

desensitize make people numb or uncaring towards something

detractor opponent, critic with low opinion

distinctive original, unusual

edify improve someone's character

editor person in charge of a newspaper, book, or magazine

feedback response to a piece of work

formula fixed way of doing things

formulaic sticking to a fixed pattern

genre category of literature (for example: humour, science fiction, horror)

glossies upmarket magazines printed on shiny paper

insatiable bottomless, never-ending

intense strongly emotional

juvenile childish, immature

media means of communication (for example: TV, radio, cinema, newspapers)

merchandise goods, e.g. toys and games, produced to tie in with the release of a film or book

production department that deals with the way a book or magazine is laid out and put together, rather than the content (text)

proof-reading reading through and checking an early printed version of the text to get rid of any problems or mistakes

rejection being turned down or refused something

royalties payments made to an author for each book of his/hers that is sold

satanic to do with the devil

simultaneously at the same time

spoof hoax

stereotypical not very original, lacking in character

stocking receiving books from a publisher and displaying them in a shop

stocks and shares the business of financial dealers, e.g. on Wall Street

substitute teacher a teacher who fills in for another teacher who is away or sick

target readership readers of the age for whom a book is intended

writer's block a problem some writers experience, where they find they cannot produce work as usual because they don't feel creative

INDEX

Arthur, Joe 9, 13, 21, 53

The Baby-sitter 33, 34-5
Bananas 23, 25, 28-9
Blind Date 32-3

Captain Anything 16-17
cliff-hangers 4, 6, 13

Eureeka's Castle 30, 31

Fear Street 4, 25, 36-7, 42, 43, 45
Feiwel, Jean 32

Goosebumps 4, 5, 25, 26-7, 38-41, 42, 43, 44-5, 49-50

Goosebumps TV series 5, 44

How To Be Funny 24-5

It Came From Ohio! 9, 13, 15, 29, 53

Junior Scholastic magazine 21-2

Maniac magazine 29
merchandising 6, 41, 44

New York 18, 19

Ohio State University 14, 15

Parachute Press, Inc. 29

Rudin, Ellen 23-4

Scholastic, Inc. 22, 23, 25, 28-9, 32, 33
Soft Drink Industry magazine 20-1
Stine, Bill (brother) 8, 15
Stine, Matt (son) 26, 27, 43

Stine, R.L.
  becomes self-employed 29-30
  birth of son 26
  college life 14-15
  devises *Fear Street* 36-7
  devises *Goosebumps* 38-9
  early childhood and schooldays 8-13
  and *Eureeka's Castle* 30, 31
  first jobs 16, 18-19, 20-3
  first writing attempts 12, 13
  launches *Bananas* 23
  marries 21
  moves to New York 18
  opinions about his books 6-7, 46-7, 48-51
  publishes first book 24-5
  publishes first horror story 19
  writes for adults 42-3
  writes first scary book 32-3
Sundial 14, 15
Superstitious 42-3

Thurber, James 11, 14, 31

Waldhorn, Jane 20, 21, 23, 29, 36, 38
Waricha, Joan 29, 36, 38